Shut up and eat!

How to quietly become a triplitarian

Copyright 2019 Nathan Bigman

Introduction

There's only one group of people who are more annoying than people who talk nonstop about what they eat, and that, of course, is the group of people who talk nonstop about running, biking, and working out.

I've sat through too many meals where the conversation centers on Western food obsessions. It's everybody, all of the time, talking about why they don't eat meat, why they do eat meat, how they feel bad about eating chicken but eat it anyway, how they're vegetarians but they eat fish (which by the way, makes them not vegetarians). It's enough to drive one mad.

So, in a moment of exasperation, I vowed to express my frustration, my ennui, and my opinion, in the hopes of convincing everyone I know, and everyone I don't know, that there are more interesting things to talk about. I also created a simple tool to organize your approach to food, so that you can quietly, in the privacy of your own home, discuss this with yourself, or with someone who has a high tolerance level for your food obsession. This might stop you from discussing it with me.

I came to this topic with strong opinions, and bits of knowledge gained over the years from reading article after article and watching show after show about what's good and what's bad for your health, for your soul, for the environment, and for the palate. I listened to my father, a conscientious physician, track over several decades the discussions about the health effects of cholesterol, or of vitamin C, and watched him wave his hands dismissively when an outrageous and definitive claim was made.

I studied science for many years, and while I learned scientific principles, I also learned how to be skeptical.

This book is a result of that training, that skepticism, and some light research. However, the point of this book is not to be authoritative in any way, but to be **not** authoritative in **every** way. You should own your personal food philosophy, and use it to create policies that guide what you eat. It should not be dictated by me, by a health magazine, or by a news report that starts "A recent scientific study has shown...". It should not be influenced by your friends. The only authority that should be involved in the establishment of your approach to food, is a medical authority, which is a nice segue into...

Disclaimer: in real life I play a guy who plays a guy who said he once knew a guy who played a doctor's friend on television. Don't accept anything I say as medical advice – get that from your friend who had 6 months of medical school, or from the flakiest medical site you can find on the Internet. **Seriously, folks**, get some proper, professional medical advice about your diet, not from this book and not from the Internet.

"A Recent Scientific Study Has Shown" can also be referred to by the acronym, ARSSHS.

So now get ready as I go on and on about why we should stop talking about what we eat. But as a special treat, I'm going to give you a simple geometrical construct to define, if only momentarily, your food policy. Here's a spoiler: it's a triangle! Once you adopt the triangle to define your approach to food, you can proudly (but quietly) proclaim that you're a triplitarian, and end the conversation about food. But you have to hang on until the very end. Curiosity piqued? Read on!

Talking about food

How did we become so obsessed with what we eat? A large part of it is that we can afford to. By "we", I mean those of us in the Western world who have the luxury of doing so. By global standards we are the well-off, the well-to-do, the wealthy. No matter what kind of car we drive or where we live, we're still better off than the millions of people who have to scrounge for food every day to avoid starving. For those people, the only obsession can be with *finding* food – choice doesn't enter the equation.

A 2017 United Nations Food and Agriculture Organization estimate (http://www.fao.org/state-of-food-security-nutrition) suggests that approximately 815 million people are currently suffering from hunger across the globe. That estimate comes with a definition of hunger, and it's not that feeling you get when you walk into your local multiplex and smell the popcorn. Hunger is when you don't have enough food to eat, to the point where you suffer from malnutrition.

　　Here's a fun linguistic fact to know and share. According to the World Health Organization (http://www.who.int/features/qa/malnutrition/en/), *malnutrition*, in our ever-more-politically-correct-and-scientifically-accurate-as-well-as-rich-and-overfed culture, just means bad nutrition. So, malnutrition can refer to eating too much, which is now called *overnutrition*, or eating too little, which is called *undernutrition*. In other words, our feckless fat people have taken over the word malnutrition and have made it their own – another triumph of Western culture.

　　I remember watching a film in my Anthropology class as a freshman at Wayne State University in Detroit. The subject was an African tribe, and I apologize to the tribe for not recalling its name. In the one scene that I remember, a young boy is picking through the brush and finds a big, fat, juicy grub. He eats it on camera in a tight shot, and his smile remains with me to this day. There's nothing like the face of a kid eating a Hershey bar – except for the face of that kid eating a grub. I've never eaten a grub, but if I had to, and I didn't have access to something better, perhaps I'd consider it a treat, though my smile wouldn't be as broad. Of course, it's possible that those grubs are objectively delicious. They are obviously subjectively delicious. There's no arguing about taste, as they say.

> I have a friend who traveled to India on business for a technology firm, and discovered that thousands of children in Mumbai skipped school to spend their entire day picking through garbage to find food. For them, spending the day this way was the only way to stay alive. My friend quit his job and started Gabriel Project Mumbai (https://www.gabrielprojec

tmumbai.org/), *an organization dedicated to providing lunch to more than 1,000 of these children. The children have only one commitment - they must attend school.*

As Westerners who have access to food in a package on a shelf, we're able to avoid the grubs if we choose, and most of us so choose. We have the luxury of worrying about carbs, sugar, gluten, MSG, nuts, peanuts, dairy, saturated fats, and total fat content. We can survive as pescatarians, vegetarians, and vegans — or at least some of the hardier among us can. And so, we take our stand based on health or ethics, moral considerations, or what's trendy and cool, and spend inordinate amounts of effort and money to remain healthy on our controlled diets. Alternatively, we throw caution and ethical considerations to the wind, and eat what tastes good.

Grubs are low in carbs, contain no MSG, and are

gluten-free. And you can't beat the price.

Other than the health impacts of these fads, the end result for many of us is...boredom. Boredom with what we're eating is bad enough. But the boredom of listening to everyone talk about what they eat and why they eat what they're eating and how often they eat it is worse. We have to listen to it while they're searching for recipes, before they shop for food, while they pay for food, while they prepare the food, when they serve the food, before they eat, while they eat, and after they eat. They regale us with tales of where they bought the asparagus and that it was local, non-GMO, and organic, or what butcher sold which kind of meat, was it free-range, was it grass-fed. We read about it in their mail, their texts, on Facebook and in their tweets. Then, we can read about it in a magazine. Throw in an article about marathon training and your insomnia is cured.

Mind you, there's nothing terrible about talking about food and how it was prepared. Food can be interesting to talk about, in the right circumstances and to the right degree. The problem is the conversation about why and how we make our food choices, and the health implications. Seriously, do you want to talk about fatty deposits on your arteries while you're eating? Apparently, you do, because you're driving every one of your relatives and friends nuts about it. And some strangers. And the waitress.

So, let's eat better, and talk about it less. The only question is, what is "better"? The answer is...there is no answer. Each person must decide on their own what the best food route to take is. And then, they should shut up about it. Hey - I'm talking to you. Pay attention! We're not interested, and we don't care.

It's true. When you talk about what you eat and why, if you spend more than fifteen seconds on the subject, you're boring. Also, you may have a personality disorder in which you believe that everything that comes out of your mouth, including descriptions of what goes into your mouth, is interesting. I say this as an expert – it's taken me decades to realize that I'm not as interesting as I think, but now I know.

If you're on a personal crusade to limit your intake of…anything, go ahead. But just because that crusade has religious meaning for you, don't expect the rest of us to be interested in helping you, joining you, or listening to you talk about it. Be miserable on your own, please. What we eat affects how we feel emotionally, how we feel physically, the condition of our bodies, our energy levels, the luster of our hair…you name it. And what we eat is a decision we make as individuals, and sometimes, as a family, but outside the four walls of our homes, we need to lay off the grinding discussion. Talk about something less off-putting, like that patch of flaky skin that won't go away no matter how much you pick at it.

The goal of this book is to help you find a comfort zone for your food consumption habits and define it succinctly, and to convince you to keep it to yourself. More so, this book helps you create that zone by using geometry. Intriguing, I know.

Once you've found your food comfort zone, the only conversation you should have about how you eat is the one in which you recommend to your friend that they read this book and become a triplitarian. And don't lend them your copy, make sure they buy their own.

Food consumer types

There are several, well-defined types of food consumers. You know them already, but let's describe them anyway, just so that we're all comfortable with the right definitions – mine. Most food consumers eat a certain way and make sure that you know it. They talk about it incessantly. And if you eat at their house, with each mouthful of their food you'll also get an earful of Oh God Who Cares. True, you can always get up and leave, but only if you want to wind up with no friends.

Omnivores

These people eat everything, and rarely talk about it. Bring on the fish, fowl, and beef, fruits and vegetables, dairy products, nut and grains. Their eating philosophy is boring and I mean that as a compliment. They eat meat, but it's not the end-all and be-all of their existence. On the other hand, their food can be interesting, though that doesn't mean that we want to have a conversation about it. Usually, these people are pretty reasonable about food choice conversations, but they can also get noisy, particularly when they're on the defensive.

Carnivores

Have you heard of the Carnivore Club? You can find a company of that name on the Internet, which is no big surprise – you can find everything on the Internet. But I speak not of that company but of a local club in my town. Once a month a member of the club hosts a barbecue in which all kinds of fowl and beast are grilled and served, in vast quantities. Fish need not apply.

Why would such a club exist? For starters, the members are mostly men. I'm going to go out on a limb here and posit that these guys feel threatened by the growing popularity and coolness of vegetarianism and veganism, and are trying to make a statement about the legitimacy and desirability of eating meat. They may feel insecure about their willing consumption of beings that are dead, and figure that it's best to counter that insecurity by standing in the town square and yelling about their love of meat, spewing grease from their mouths all the while.

I won't go so far as to suggest that they're also insecure about their masculinity or heterosexuality, nor will I paint for you a mental picture of hairy men in Fred Flintstone onesies carrying clubs in one hand and joints of beef or mutton in the other. Or you may be imagining Henry the 8th with his fist clutching a turkey leg. But that's you, I would never suggest such a thing.

There's certainly a range of carnivorism, or carnivoricity. Carnivoraciousness. At one end reside the squeamish carnivores, who are put off by the idea of the pens, the slaughter, the spurting blood, and the death throes. At the other end are the he-men and she-women who, in their quest for flesh, come close to tearing the limb off of a live animal.

My point – there are people who love meat, eat meat, and think that it's perfectly acceptable ethically to kill for food. And they can be as annoying as the most religious vegan, because they talk nonstop about how much they like meat and how they don't think it's wrong to kill creatures to eat them. And they're not going away.

Don't worry, there's a section about vegetarians, and they get theirs, too.

Pescatarians

No, not Episcopalians, and not Presbyterians, though there could be some overlap. Mostly, these are people who like to call themselves vegetarians because it's hip, but they eat fish for various reasons:

- They have ethical issues with eating meat
- They think it's less cruel to kill fish than to kill cows and chickens
- It might be healthier than other flesh alternatives
- Tuna sandwiches are delicious
- They're hungry

Full disclosure – I was once one of these. And I did think for a while that it was better to kill fish than to kill chickens. Now, I'm pretty sure I was wrong. I guess I liked the idea of vegetarianism, but couldn't stick to it without eating fish. But why would one think that it's better to kill fish than to kill chickens? Do fish feel less pain than chickens? Do shellfish? Sometimes, a gesture toward ethical practice is just insipid.

    Perhaps it's better to kill caged chickens than wild fish. Which life has more value? Which death is more tragic or horrifying? Then you can consider wild fish versus free-range chickens, or farm-raised fish versus caged chickens. Where would beef fit into the picture? While these ethical dilemmas continue to reverberate, there are people in the world who would kill for a bite to eat and would be right to do so. But now even *I'm* getting hungry, so we'll continue the discussion of ethics later.

> *There are some who justify eating shellfish because shellfish don't feel pain. There are some who justify eating shellfish because shellfish don't appreciate musical theatre. While the latter claim is certainly true, the former is debatable, according to a*

survey of current science in Wikipedia (*https://en.wikipedia.org/wiki/Pain_in_crustaceans*), the lazy man's research solution.

Vegetarians

Here's a quandary. How many types of vegetarians are there? It would be easier to answer the other critical question: how many vegetarians does it take to screw in a light bulb?

- Two. One to twist in the lightbulb and one to check the ingredients.
- Four. One on whom they can fob off the unavoidable task while the other three anguish over how many animals were killed by the habitat destruction necessary to extract the minerals required to manufacture the bulb.

Hilarious. Thank you, Internet, for enabling me to research vegetarian light bulb jokes.

Here are some types of vegetarians:

- Ovo-vegetarian – Eggs, no dairy. Omelet ok, hold the cheese.

- Lacto-vegetarian – Dairy, no eggs. Toasted cheese is fine, make sure there's no egg in the bread.
- Ovo-lacto – Eggs and dairy. Cheese omelet, mushrooms optional.
- Vegan – no animal products. No omelet, no toasted cheese.

Some vegans won't eat honey. I have respect for the non-honey vegans because I think they're crazy and might kill me if I disrespect them. I also suspect that some vegans would prefer not to be thought of as a subset of vegetarians, because vegetarians still exploit animals for milk, eggs, and honey. Many vegans won't wear leather, or wool. Presumably silk is out of the question. So are synthetics, which are made from petroleum, which came from dinosaurs, though I may be a little presumptuous about vegan behavior. However, now that I've said it, vegans should probably stick to cotton and linen.

Did you hear the one about the vegetarian who

insisted that his eggs come from vegetarian chickens? That's not a joke – there are people like that. How they keep the chickens from eating bugs, worms and maggots is beyond me. Also, preventing chickens from eating those things seems unfair to the chicken. In fact, one might even say that it's cruel.

For each of those types of vegetarians, there are many people who choose that diet for ethical reasons, but there are also some who choose that diet for health reasons. That is, they don't care about the beasts, they just think it's healthier to not eat meat, chicken, fish, and possibly dairy products. For some people, consumption of one of those animal products actually makes them ill.

Vegetarianism, and veganism in particular, are demanding food-styles, since there's a tremendous level of effort involved in ensuring that one consumes the right foods to, you know, stay alive and healthy. This is an even greater issue for children, who have extra nutritional requirements for growth.

Here's a non-scientific anecdote about the health benefits of veganism. I know a family with four children, the oldest of whom is a very vocal vegan, while the three younger children are also vegan, but less vocal, at least for now. Two of the children have had serious, digestive-system-related illnesses. I haven't reviewed their medical charts, but have to wonder. I suspect that some people have the constitution for veganism, and some do not.

Most importantly, if your avoidance of meat, eggs, or dairy is important to you, don't assume that the rest of us want to hear about it. You folks are really, truly, the most vocal about your food preferences. I understand that you feel a need to proselytize so as to save the lives of animals. You may also believe that production of meat, from raising the livestock to slaughtering and processing it, is harmful to the environment. But there is a time and place for those discussions, and that time and place is not *every* time and every place. It's irritating, and turns your audience against you. Lead quietly by personal example, and you'll make the world a better place by taking up less of everyone else's time and space.

Vegans

These are not a subset of vegetarians. No way. Vegetarians are evil and exploit cows, chickens and beans. Vegans don't. Except for the beans. Also, vegans tend to be horrible to humans, chewing our ears off about the horrors of honey consumption. Stop. Just stop.

Chronotarians

No, not people who eat clocks. These are those who have strict rules about when to eat:

- Breakfast is the most important meal of the day
- Never eat breakfast
- Eat two big meals a day, that is all
- Snack all day
- Fast two days a week

As individuals, you have a right to believe any of these rules, or all of them. As a group, just realize that everyone else hates you.

Phobics

Some of my best friends are phobics, a word I just made up. For the sake of language purists (some of my best friends are language purists), these friends have phobias, and are phobic. The phobic friends fear a food substance, or several food substances, and are also acutely aware of alliteration. Typical food fears frequently found among my phobic friends are carbohydrates — especially sugar, and also gluten, MSG, and margarine. To a large extent, these are driven by fads, some of which are in turn driven by the ARSSHS affect. Fad or no, the primary result is fear of foodstuffs.

Phobics should not be confused with people who are particularly picky. The picky can also ruin a planned meal, but they're not food-fearful, they just don't like a lot of things. Too bad for them, right?

> *I used to hate cilantro. I then went through a special program*

coordinated by my wife, in which I received positive rewards for eating cilantro. And now, I like cilantro to the point that I miss it acutely in certain dishes. Yes, I was treated like a lab rat, but my culinary life was enriched.

Also, I find that I eat more cheese than I used to. Rat much?

Carbophobes

These people are everywhere. Apparently, they forgot the years-long period when we were all told to eat pasta as a low-fat food – or was I the only one who got that message? The extremists in this group avoid carbs altogether in an effort to lose weight – and they succeed, by completely screwing up their bodies' metabolism.

Doctor Robert C Atkins, inventor of the famous eponymous diet, died from a slip and fall in 2003. This is probably because he was eating an unbalanced diet.

Too soon?

Sugarphobes

These are the folks who believe that sugar (a particularly nefarious carb) is the devil's spawn, the source of all health problems, addictive, akin to heroin and cocaine, and the cause of all of society's problems. Sadly, this is all true, but mostly in the US. Nearly everywhere else, if sugar is available, people seem to be coping, enjoying it in moderation, and are happy about it.

What I like best about the path that sugar fear is taking in the US, is that there is societal momentum toward the regulation of sugar at the same time as marijuana is becoming legal. I like to imagine the day when you can no longer get a marijuana brownie because the *sugar* is illegal.

Glutenophobes

People with celiac disease cannot eat gluten. For some reason, though, many people who don't have celiac disease have decided that gluten is poisonous. About 1% of the US population has celiac disease. About 30% of the US population avoids gluten. Though it's entirely possible that some people are sensitive to gluten without having celiac disease, that 29% difference is more likely the result of a food fad than of good science or dietary necessity.

See a doctor if you think gluten is causing you to have health issues. Learn more from the Celiac Disease Foundation website (https://celiac.org/blog/2014/02/9-things-you-should-know-before-going-gluten-free/).

MSGphobes

MSG gives some people terrible, incapacitating headaches. For everyone else, it just makes food tasty, by adding umami. Umami is considered the fifth flavor distinguished by your taste buds, in addition to salt, sweet, sour, and bitter. It's the savory flavor we taste in meats and chicken soup.

Have you ever seen a list of foods that trigger migraines? Those lists include red wine, cheese, chocolate, and citrus fruit — not just MSG. Why has MSG been so specifically maligned? Is it because it's a powder, like sugar? Maybe I should start a movement that eschews every food substance that comes in powder form: MSG, sugar, flour, salt, baking powder, baking soda, powdered spices, corn starch, corn meal, and that weird powder at the bottom of the cereal box that turns to glue when exposed to milk.

Margarinophobes

I don't like margarine and avoid eating it. It just doesn't taste as good as butter or olive oil. But some people are a little crazed about the evils of margarine, which is not surprising. Not because margarine is so horrible, but because people are crazy, without exception. Sorry.

The other day someone told me that margarine cannot be digested by the human gut. That can't be right. If you moved to a diet heavy in margarine it might affect your health, but it would also make you fat. That wouldn't be true if margarine were indigestible.

The indigestible and calorie-free substitute for oil was Olean. It was so indigestible that it gave people horrible diarrhea, which makes perfect sense if you think about it. In fact, even if you don't think about it, it still makes sense. But better not to think about it.

GMOphobes

Genetically modified organisms, GMOs, include some amazing things, like rice with extra vitamin C in it. Also, the modified genes get stuck on the legs of bees and are transferred to birds, who poop it on humans, who grown an extra brain and tentacles and take over the world.

Frankly, I'd worry more about pesticides, but to each his own.

Ethics, the pinnacle of the triplitarian triangle

The ethical considerations of our consumption policy belong at the top of our triangle. Needless to say, it's an obtuse topic, so let's dive right in.

On second thought, let's wade in slowly, test the waters, and hesitate along the way.

I once asked a friend if he was a vegetarian and he asked "Ethically or in practice?" That friend makes a decision about ethics every time he shops, eats in or eats out: should he have a hamburger, or pasta with tomato sauce (vegan), or pasta in cream sauce (vegetarian) or in cream sauce with salmon (pescatarian)? Or, maybe he only considers the question every few months, but doesn't agonize over it while his hamburger gets cold, or his salad gets warm.

Even more likely, he probably only thinks about it when some idiot asks him. I should have left him alone.

Eating Flesh

If you're going to eat beef, pork, fowl, snakes, cockroaches or grubs, what ends up on your plate was once alive. Some people don't think about it at all, or think about it and conclude that this is fine. Others stand in the town square with signs that say "Beef is murder" and horrifying photos of animals on their way to slaughter. Presumably, they don't eat meat, unless they don't mind the murder aspect.

On those extremes, there's no ongoing grappling over the question of the ethics of being a carnivore. But those of us who are uncomfortable on the extremes, and normal in every other way, generally do grapple.

The Food Chain

In deciding whether to eat meat, one should consider the food chain. There is such a thing, and it doesn't bother us that lions eat zebras, that bats eat mosquitoes, that bears eat honey and salmon (but not usually together, though that could be good with the right seasoning). As humans, historically and biologically, are we not meant to eat meat, and dairy, and eggs? Witness aboriginals, or any human group that is suffering from malnutrition – they'll eat anything that will improve their odds of survival. It's difficult to say that it's unethical for humans to eat flesh when it seems to be part of nature's plan. We even have the teeth for it, and when those fall out, we can get new ones.

So, one could posit that humans have a right, granted by nature, to eat meat – the same right that nature grants to lions.

On the other hand, perhaps because we are able to consider the ethical implications of our actions we are obligated to change our behavior based on those implications. That is, to rise above our nature in order to prove or improve our humanity.

   But who are "we"? Are humans as a species required by some ethical consideration to rise above and to eschew meat consumption? Some humans obviously feel that need, and some obviously don't. From a purely practical perspective, humanity as a whole is unlikely to ever become vegetarian, which makes this an ethical decision of the heart for an individual. Either you feel a need to be more morally sophisticated than other beasts, or you don't. If you do, but don't act on that feeling, it's time to give that more thought. No need to discuss it with everyone you know, of course. Just to remind you – we might care a little, but we're not that interested.

> *A parallel could perhaps be found between our refinement of our food consumption and our refinement of sexual*

relationships, though I believe I'll save that discussion for my next book.

Fleshy choices

You may know a pescatarian. Some pescatarians avoid pork, beef and fowl for health reasons, but there are some who do so for ethical reasons. When considering this behavior, some might ask, "Huh?"

Is it ethically preferable to eat fish than to eat chicken? On what basis would one reach that conclusion? Would it have some kind of relationship to the intelligence of the creature? I suppose we could measure the intelligence of species and then rank them in terms of ethical edibility. Would you then rank all members of a species as a group, or as individuals? If as individuals, some humans could be in trouble. Equally problematic, we'd have to give intelligence tests to every chicken.

Let's say that there is some ethical release for eating "lower species". Then, you could conceive of an eating philosophy that encourages humans to not eat other creatures, and to draw lines of increasing evil as one moved from eating single-celled members of the animal kingdom, up to mollusks, fish, birds, and mammals. Or you could look at it in a more positive light, with the human consumers of animals being the most evil, and becoming ever more righteous as they forgo the "higher" animals, and, for animal flesh, eat only…grubs.

Are cuteness or beauty counted among the ethical considerations? That can get messy, given how subjective beauty is. In the western world we wouldn't eat dogs or turtles or chipmunks or peacocks. On the other hand, cows have gorgeous eyes, and we eat them with gusto. In China, eat a dog to stay warm in the winter. Sole is a beautiful fish, before it's caught killed, scaled, and fried. At that point it's just delicious. A butterfly is about as advanced a creature as a cockroach, but it's a little more handsome. Once again, if we did this assessment on an individual level, some humans…well, you know who you are.

Does the environment in which the creatures live come into play? One could reasonably posit that from the standpoint of sustainability, and human responsibility to not deplete wild species or cause them to go extinct, that we're better off eating farm-raised creatures, whether fish, fowl, or large beast.

> *For those of you who are not counting, I've used the word "posit" three times. Four, now. My mother must be so proud.*

Should we consider living conditions of those farm-raised creatures? It seems kinder to eat animals that lived reasonably while they lived. There's no point in causing the pig to suffer in addition to turning him into pepperoni, right? This is actually a relatively easy and practical ethical stance to take, if you are a consumer of flesh.

Such a choice **is** more expensive. However, if you choose to be careful about the source of the flesh you buy and consume, assuring some minimal standard of care for the creatures, you create economic pressure on the producers of the flesh to be kinder to their beasts. Eventually, if there's enough pressure, there will be more producers of "kind flesh", and the prices will drop. I say this just in case you're worried about the cost to you more than you worry about kindness to animals. And cost may be a real issue for you. Even if you live in a land with a grub-free diet, that doesn't mean you don't have to budget for food cost.

Where does hunting fit in? Beats me. It would be hard for me personally to put a bullet, or arrow, or even a hook into some creature in order to eat it. On the other hand, there's something to be said for the idea that if you're not willing to take the animal's life with your own hands, you should not be eating it. Meat doesn't come from a supermarket, neatly packaged. It comes from an animal with a face. This even holds true for snail meat (it's not really a face, but they have eyes and a mouth).

At the very least, pay attention to the chicken, turkey, and livestock trucks you see barreling down the road to the slaughterhouse. There's nothing like seeing a flatbed truck loaded with hundreds of cages, each cage containing eight chickens. They head out on the highway no matter how hot the sun, how wet the rain. I once saw a stack of those chicken cages sitting in 100+ degree weather outside a slaughterhouse, and frankly, it was horrifying. That was without seeing them get their throats slit. Feel a little vegetarianism coming on?

If you want to eat meat, be aware of the edible-animal life cycle before you take a bite. Then, if you like, dig in.

Ethical Extremes

You can take your ethical approach to the very edges of reason, either respecting animal rights to an extreme that is beyond ridicule, or completely ignoring the suffering creatures we eat.

For example, the refusal to make use of any animal product or by-product could box you into some ethically-bounded corners:

- If you refuse to use animal products, would you eat vegetables fertilized with goat manure? What if they were free-range goats?
- If you don't want to eat vegetables that benefited from animal manure, would you eat those that were fertilized with petrochemicals? If so, you're benefiting from the death of thousands of dinosaurs. And if you reject that usage, then you probably can't drive a car. Or ride a bus. Or use electricity if

it's generated by burning oil or coal.
- If it's okay to use those petroleum –sourced chemicals because the dinosaurs died a natural death, not at the hands of man, would you eat a chicken that died of old age?
- Would you eat vegetables treated with pesticides? I'm not speaking of any risk that pesticides pose to you, I speak of the millions of insect lives snuffed out by those chemicals.
- Perhaps a more realistic question is how the production of all of those petrochemicals and their impact on the environment affect the ethical status of the final food product? True, that's an environmental consideration, not an animal-resource consideration, but it should probably still come into play, as we'll discuss below.

- How about bee labor in fertilizing flowers to produce fruit? Is it right to take advantage of that labor?

Do those questions sound ridiculous? They're only an exaggeration of positions that I've been exposed to in my conversations with vegetarians and vegans.

Coming at it from an opposite point of view, there are some food practices that smash right through a reasonable approach to ethical food considerations. Two obvious ones are the forced feeding of geese to produce foie gras, and the caging of calves to create veal. To a vegetarian these might seem like a small move on the scale of ethical considerations. However, to an omnivore or carnivore who has come to terms with the idea that it's permissible for humans to eat animal flesh, the torture of animals prior to killing them should still be beyond the pale.

This isn't a logical conclusion, but an emotional one, yet it still bears weight.

Admittedly, the sliding ethical scale might pull in some other practices as being unacceptable. For example, is throwing a live lobster into a pot of boiling water "over the top" ethically? If so, how is that worse than taking a live carp out of a tank, smashing it on the head, and 70 seconds later, handing a tray of ground carp to a customer? I know it's a Rosh Hashanah tradition, but come on, folks.

There are no obvious answers once you move away from the extremes, but it's worthwhile to ask the questions, to not take lightly the ethics of our consumption habits.

Environmental Ethics

Ethical edibility is not just about eating meat. It's also about considering how and where our food is produced, and the impact of our choices on the environment. I have to restate that this is an issue primarily for people who have access to plenty of food. Without that reminder, this book would be too short.

There's no way around the fact that every human on the face of the planet has an impact on the environment. And why not? Every animal and every plant has an impact on the environment, for better or for worse. The human impact is amplified because of our ability to use tools to magnify our power and to defend ourselves against most predators (the notable exception being other humans), and to create pharmaceuticals and medical procedures to protect ourselves from pathogens and rescue us from injury. This has resulted in a huge increase in our population, at the expense of the environment around us. And thanks to our big, science-filled brains, we're able to provide food to support (much of) our huge populations. That results, of course, in gargantuan lots full of shitting pigs, and the resultant environmental damage.

So, as part of our ethical considerations, we should think about how what we eat affects the environment. For example, we might choose to eat more vegetarian-like, because it takes a lot of vegetable matter to produce a small quantity of consumable flesh. Or, we might choose to eat organic foods because they don't use chemicals in the production of that food. That could be seen as a health benefit, not just an ethical one, nonetheless, keeping chemicals out of soil and groundwater is a good idea. So, if someone doesn't believe that fertilizers and pesticides harm their health, or they believe that they do cause harm to their health but don't care, they could still make an ethical choice to eat organic foods in order to do less harm to the environment.

As Westerners with choices, we can also consider the overall cost of producing, shipping, and packaging our food. For example, how much energy is used in the growing, packaging, and shipping of what we eat? What are the aftereffects of our food consumption? Even without ignoring the issue of killing a creature to eat it, how do you decide if it's worse to eat a locally-raised chicken, or to drink a bottle of water that was shipped to Seattle from Atlanta, or an ear of corn sent from Florida to Michigan?

There are other, more direct environmental implications. What is the environmental impact of raising a cow or pig for meat? How about the effect of tons of fertilizers and pesticides used to grow grains, fruits, and vegetables?

These are complicated equations, but they are part of deciding what kind of consumer of food you want to be. Even if you can't answer the questions, considering them can help you find your comfort space for food.

Food Waste

One of the less-complicated ways of helping the environment is avoiding food waste. Food waste may be a bigger problem than the environmental costs of agriculture or the ethics of eating what was once alive.

Simply put, if you waste food, you've committed several crimes. It's easy to understand why it's horrible to toss the flesh of a creature into the garbage. On a lesser scale, the same holds true for agricultural products. You've taken all the energy, effort, water, and fertilizers used to produce that food, and you've thrown them in the trash.

If you have trouble imagining this waste, picture the resources and work that went into growing the wheat for the loaf of bread, or the apple you munch on after eating your PB&J sandwich. Start with the farmer driving a tractor to plow the fields, fertilize the crops and to harvest the grain or produce. Every time you eat an apple or a slice of bread, you're consuming the literal and metaphorical fruit of that energy use. If your food comes from far away, for example, a grape that came from Chile to Ohio, because we Americans think it's normal to eat grapes in the winter, then the trucks and ships and planes that brought you that grape have also invested their energy in it. A certain amount of energy to produce food is a reasonable investment in our needs, though the grape from Chile is more than a little over the top. However, taking that energy investment and tossing it in the trash is tragic.

And it kills me to imagine the wine grapes, and the harvest, the fermentation, the storage and the shipping, of the glass of wine that goes down the drain. True, some of that wine should never have been produced in the first place, but it still pains me, and it should pain you. And if it's good wine, that should cause true heartache.

There are ways to mitigate the amount of food waste and the effects of food waste.

First, do your best to buy only what you will eat, and pay attention to the food you've stored. Don't buy so many fruits and vegetables that a portion of them inevitably rots on your counter or in your refrigerator drawers. Don't cook more of a dish than you expect to eat before it goes bad. And don't forget about your leftovers – eat them!

A less effective mitigation to food waste is to make sure that the food that escapes your attention and ends up rotting finally goes into a compost bin. At least, that way, it doesn't get buried in a landfill.

> *When I was a pescatarian, I strictly avoided beef and chicken...until Wednesday night. That is, if the leftover chicken from Friday was still in the refrigerator on Wednesday night, I knew that nobody was going to eat it and that it was going to go in the garbage. The same held true for cooked chicken that had been in the freezer for more than several weeks. I would eat that chicken, and though it*

distressed me emotionally (I got over it) and gastronomically (because it tasted pretty bad), I knew that there was one thing worse than killing a beast in order to eat it, and that was killing a beast and then throwing it in the garbage.

Food waste is a phenomenon peculiar to food-rich societies. We should be putting a higher value on every bit of food that passes before us. We should buy less, and eat every morsel of what we buy.

I have a friend who lives in Nepal. They milk the cows and goats in the morning, drink some of the milk, make some cheese, and sell the excess to the neighbors. By the time they go to bed, it's all been consumed. That is one reason why they don't have a refrigerator – they don't need one.

The other reason is that they only have a few reliable hours of electricity a day.

Reducing our impact

Let's look at the peripheral environmental costs of our food – the energy involved in producing it, and the packaging that it comes in. As with most environmental issues, a little common sense goes a long way.

Start by buying less packaged food, and food with less packaging. For example, breakfast cereal in a bag creates less trash than breakfast cereal in a box, which is also in a bag, in a box, which gets to the store in a bigger box. The energy to produce the bag is also likely to be smaller than the energy used to produce the box (with a bag in it). Usually those bagged cereals are generic, but if enough of us purchase the bagged stuff, perhaps Kellogg's, Post, Nestle and General Mills would get the message.

It's also true that larger packages use less packaging material. That is, one large bottle of liquid detergent comes in more-efficient packaging than 2 small bottles.

Once you've purchased the package and consumed the contents, there is usually an option to recycle. Remember, though, that there are also energy costs associated with recycling. Let's consider, again, the cereal box. It's possible, even likely, that the box is made from recycled paper, and the box you bought can be turned into a new box, thus saving part of a tree. So, take the box to the recycling center down the block. If you walk there, great. If you drive there, that's an energy cost. The box sits in the bin for a while, and when the bin is full, a huge truck, burning diesel fuel and belching fumes, comes to pick up the box.

Your box then goes to the paper recycling plant, where the machinery grinds and sorts and soaks and mashes and drains and rolls...you get the picture. A crap-load, possibly even a shit-ton, of energy goes into recycling that box. This may be more efficient than making paper out of tree that has to be cut and transported and pulped, but it's not cost-free. Recycling of paper, glass, metals and plastics uses energy and pollutes. So, it's always better to stop the cycle at the beginning and avoid the packaging as much as possible.

But you should still recycle.

Bottled Drinks – a pet peeve and a rant

A good way to avoid packaging and reduce energy use from all angles is to avoid bottled drinks of any kind. When you buy a bottle of cola, you're buying a bottle that had to be manufactured, shipped to the cola plant, filled, trucked to a distribution center, and then trucked to your local store. After you drink the cola, under the best of circumstances, that bottle gets shipped and melted and turned into a new bottle. If you consider just the fleet of trucks you launch when you buy that cola, both on the manufacturing end and on the recycling end, you're going to realize that it's wiser to just skip it.

Even worse is the purchasing of *water* in containers, whether you buy ½-liter or 5-gallon bottles. The smaller bottles have all of the same material and energy costs as the cola bottles (except for the few cents it costs to turn water into cola). The 5-gallon water bottles delivered to your home aren't much better, though those are presumably reused, not recycled. But water is heavy — think of the transportation costs!

In the Western world, perfectly good water comes out of the faucet. If you don't like the taste, add a carbon filter. You'll save money and do less environmental damage. Sending water all over the place in trucks is simply stupid and wasteful.

Environmental Wisdom

As a wise person who purchased this book, remember that no matter what you do, you're going to have impact on the environment just by virtue of your existence on Earth. That's true of any creature, though humans are particularly good at trashing our surroundings. You could argue that as residents of Earth, our impact is part of nature. Chimpanzees also use tools and that affects their level of impact on the environment – you would be hard pressed to consider that unnatural. Perhaps humanity, with all of its fumes and trash, is part of a natural cycle of growth and decay. Our population can grow and grow, and we can continue to exude fumes and create mounds of useless trash. Then, when we've exhausted all of Earth's resources and have made the air and water filthy beyond their ability to support life, the whole system will crash, humanity will mostly die out, and things can start over from the beginning. And that would be natural. But even if you consider that a natural phenomenon, it doesn't sound pleasant.

Probably the best thing you can do for the environment is to die before you have any children. I'm not recommending this, but it does give one pause, and perhaps that can spur us to be more careful about our use of resources.

Every person makes their own decisions about where to invest their effort to keep our human ecosystem running more-or-less smoothly. My recommendation is, when you make decisions about your eco-lifestyle, consider what you're leaving the next generation, and act accordingly.

A note about "just this one box". It's easy to think that the one cereal box, the one rotten peach, the one plastic bottle that you throw in the trash doesn't have any impact. But one box plus one box plus another box add up to a lot of boxes pretty quickly. Take a cereal box and fold it as compactly as you can.

Now, imagine 10 of them, 100, or 100,000 of them. If a cereal box takes up two cubic inches of space, 100,000 of them take up about 4 cubic yards. The 2.7 billion cereal boxes sold in the USA every year (according to statisticbrain.com) would, if compacted, add up to 115,740 cubic yards of cardboard. Imagine a football field full of crushed cardboard to a height of about 3400 feet. If you, and your neighbor on either side of you, use one fewer box and one fewer bottle, or makes the effort to recycle, one plus one does make a difference.

Here's one more. At the company where I work, we use about 1000 paper coffee cups per day. Over a

*300-day work year, we discard a stack of cups 1.5 kilometers tall (+ 9 cm for the first cup). That's the coffee-cup trash produced by **one** company.*

Ethical Etiquette

Compared to other issues, food etiquette seems at best, a minor consideration, and at worst, uninteresting. However, this affects us frequently and is worth mentioning.

You're at someone's house for dinner, and you forgot to tell them that you don't eat meat or chicken or fish or eggs or dairy or cocoa. This sounds like an unusual situation, because many of us are used to being asked by the host about our weird food requirements when they invite us. It's the American way. But maybe this time, you happen to be in France.

In France people eat a lot of pork. Here's a thing they do, and do well. They take a piglet, kill it, bone it, stuff it with delicious stuff, and roast it. Then they sell it by the slice. It's a stuffed-piglet cross-section! Yum.

So, you're chez your host and out comes the slice of pig. Barring religious objections to the pig (attention Jews and Moslems), do you eat the food or reject it? Rejecting it is rude, and that's an ethical violation, on a small scale. Best to eat it. If you just can't, then decline politely and have another glass of wine. One last alternative is to lecture your host about cruelty to pigs. In English we call that a faux pas, one that will drastically reduce the number and frequency of dinner invitations you receive, and justly so.

Making an ethical decision

Make the ethics of your food choice a personal decision. Consider all of the factors, then decide what you're comfortable with ethically. If you're religious, you can ask for advice from your minister, priest, imam, rabbi, pundit. Then, ignore their advice and do what you think is right. You're an adult, right? And remember – keep it to yourself.

Taste, the second point on the triplitarian triangle

With great food choices comes great responsibility – and great enjoyment. A proper, crusty baguette with loads of butter, eaten al fresco with juice or coffee, is a great way to start a day. If you can eat that baguette in the South of France on a cool, sunny morning, even better. Some might think that it's not as healthy as shredded wheat in skim milk, but others might say that if all of your food tastes like shredded wheat, you may as well lie down and die right now – though I, personally, like shredded wheat. Followed by a buttered baguette. In the South of France.

We live luxurious lives of plenty. How do I know this? Because we all spend money on books, even this one. From this fact, one can reason that we have the spare cash to buy delicacies, fine wines, and unusual scotches and bourbons. And fine imported cheeses. And rare cuts of meat.

It's true that there are people who don't care what they eat, people who don't know whether what they're eating is good or not, and people who can't afford to eat delicious food. There are also people who don't like music, but that doesn't mean there aren't others who can hear and appreciate the intricacies of a piano passage. For those who tell the difference between delicious and lousy food, and can also *afford* delicious, taste is another factor to consider when setting a food policy for yourself. This is true for a large portion of Western populations, whether or not they can afford foie gras (which I'm sure you wouldn't eat) and filet mignon every night, or any night.

Face it - omnivores have more options. People who decide to be vegan, despite their protestations, are giving up on certain flavors and textures that make food delightful. Vegetarians give up less. People with religion-based dietary restrictions (no beef, no pork, or no beef with cheese, no meat on Fridays) also restrict their pleasure.

> *My wife and I once invited a Rabbi and his family to a meal at our home. A few days before the meal we called and asked him if they had any dietary restrictions, were they vegetarian or something, and he replied, "No, keeping kosher is enough."*

When considering your food choices, balance your ethical considerations with your pleasure in eating. Similarly, balance your health considerations (with your doctor's input) against what you enjoy eating. There isn't a right approach, just your own, personal one.

Health, the third point on the triplitarian triangle

I recently went to a cardiologist to complain about the heartache I was suffering from the waste of good wine. No, that's just a joke of a particular kind (the not-funny kind). I went because of a little arrhythmia. This doctor had an app on his Android tablet, into which he input my cholesterol and triglyceride results, and maybe some other things like tobacco and alcohol habits, and then came up with a number representing the likelihood that I'd have a heart attack in the next ten years. He didn't want to tell me the number, though I think it was 6%. Not too bad, in my opinion, nonetheless he prescribed a cholesterol-lowering drug, saying that only a tiny percent of the population can control their cholesterol through diet. But you probably know someone who's trying to do so.

Now, I take the pill and eat the butter. I ate the butter before, but gave it some passing thought. Now, there's no thought.

They used to say that men who worked on offshore oil rigs had steak and eggs for breakfast, steak sandwiches for lunch, steak and potatoes for dinner, and heart attacks at 40. I guess they liked steak. Whether or not that tale is true, many of us balance health against enjoyment, on top of ethical considerations. You probably do this all of the time, even if you pause only a moment to do so before making a food choice.

Clearly there are foods that have some kind of negative impact on some portion of humanity. Two that come to your mind immediately are gluten and MSG. I didn't have to mention those; you were thinking about them already – I mentioned them in my list of phobics. If you weren't already thinking of these, I'm sorry I brought them up.

MSG was a villain for a long time because it gave some people headaches. For the sake of those people it's good that there are products that do not contain MSG, such as the chicken soup powder you can use to flavor soup. Though you have to wonder, what's in that powder? Not chicken, that's for sure.

The same holds true for gluten - there's no chicken in it. Also, there are people who are truly sickened by it, some who legitimately feel better without it, and a lot of crazy people who once heard something about gluten and flipped out, started to act as if they had celiac disease, and drove everyone around them nuts. To those people I say, don't come over for lunch.

Another villain is sugar. I think we can all agree that sugar is sweet, and some things are better sweet. There are definitely people who shouldn't eat sugar, some who should eat less, and probably some who can eat as much sugar as they want.

The problem is that every day there's a new scientific study that tells you what's going to help you live forever. Maybe it's best if you avoid sugar, eat salmon, drink one glass of red wine a day, have two squares of bitter dark chocolate, eat lots of fiber, avoid MSG, eschew gluten, shy away from nitrites... what did I forget? That is, until next week, when a new study tells you otherwise. As the old joke goes, you won't live forever, it will just seem like forever.

If you have a serious health condition that requires you to limit or eliminate salt, sugar, MSG, gluten, meat, eggs, or anything else you might be sensitive or allergic too, be vigilant, and ask those around you to help if necessary.

Don't rely on the Internet for information. That is, you can research health recommendations, but recognize that there is a difference between information published by the American Medical Association or the Mayo Clinic, and information published by Joe or Jill Blogger.

Meanwhile, here's my recipe for salmon:

Ingredients:
  One 3-ounce salmon filet
  ½ cup of red wine
  2 squares of dark, very bitter chocolate

Preparation:
  Put the salmon in a pan. Grate the chocolate over the salmon. Pour the wine. Bake at 357 degrees Fahrenheit for 19 minutes. Enjoy, if you can. Serves one crazed health nut. Tastes horrible.

A note about alcohol: Alcoholics walk among us. For an alcoholic, avoiding alcohol is not a phobia or an annoying habit, it's an important and critical need that every one of us should support. So, if someone turns down alcohol, that should be the end of the offer and there's no need to discuss it further. And if you have a friend who is an alcoholic, or even a casual acquaintance who is comfortable discussing their addiction with you, you should ask how you can help. If having a bottle of wine on the table is going to make their life more difficult, forego it for that meal.

The Triplitarian Triangle

Conveniently enough, we now have three parameters to consider when choosing a food consumption policy: health, ethics, and taste. Putting those on the points of a triangle yields the triplitarian triangle, which helps you decide and present how you lead your life of food consumption.

The triplitarian triangle looks like this:

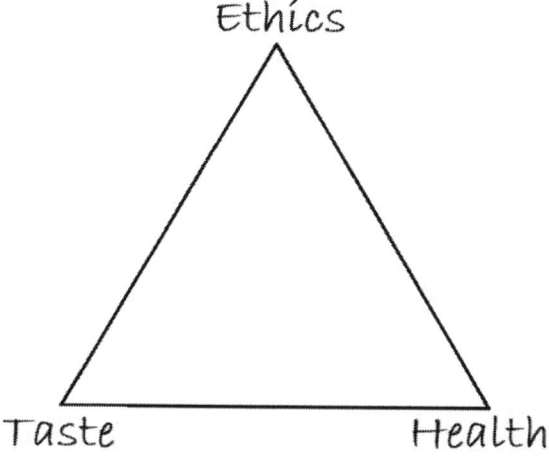

On this triangle you can plot your personal attitude toward food. By doing so you force yourself to define your attitude. You can then gauge how well you conform to your own approach in practice.

It's easiest to demonstrate how this works by considering the extremes.

For starters, take the body builder who eats only boiled protein (white meat chicken or shrimp) and drinks whey protein drinks. He doesn't care about the chicken or shrimp as creatures, and his food has no flavor, so here's where we put him. Or her.

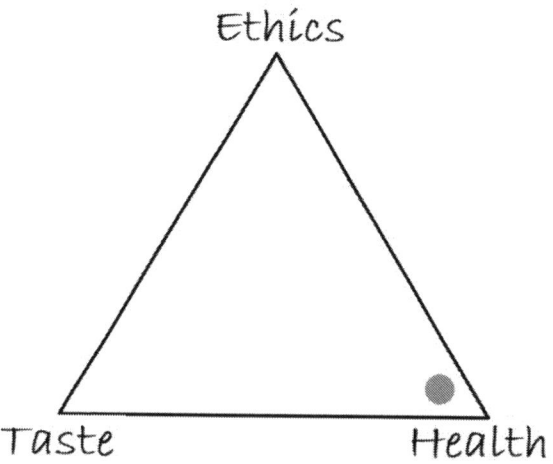

One could posit (five times, if you're still counting) that eating only boiled protein isn't that healthy. If that irks you, pretend that these people also eat rice cakes and raw broccoli.

The taste extreme is also pretty easy to plot. This person eats huge meals of beef, chicken, pork, eggs, butter, white flour, potatoes fried in lard. In my case, I'd probably have hot dogs twice a day, and merguez sausage for the third meal. My wife - cookies, chocolate, cookies that contain chocolate, and chocolate that contains cookies. These diets are all delicious, but low on the health scale, and no regard for possible ethical issues. Here they are:

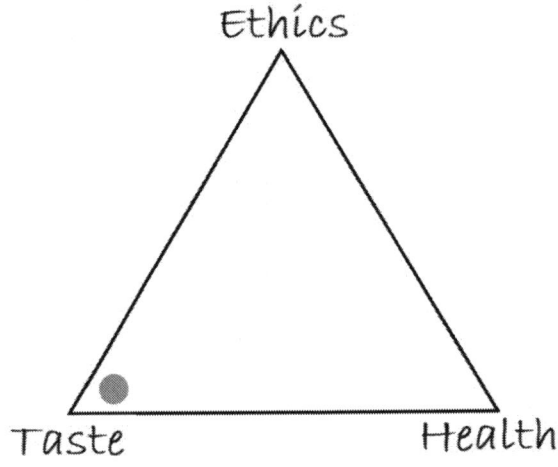

The ethics extremist is a vegan who is religious about not eating animal flesh or products, but is happy to eat any kind of meat substitute where the list of ingredients covers the entire side of a box and requires at least a Master's degree in Chemistry to understand. Voila:

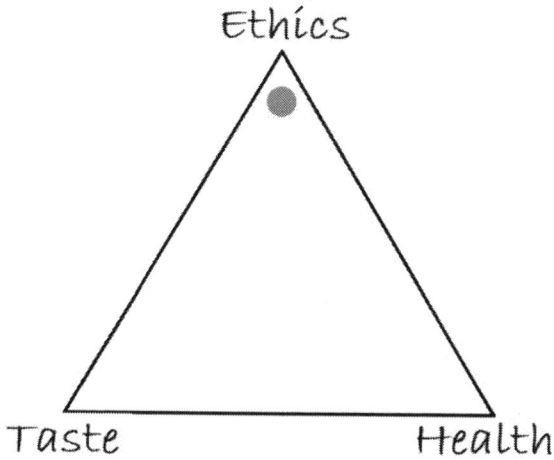

Now that we've defined some extremes, we can plot some real people who we know, some of whom we like, and some of whom we barely tolerate.

Here's a vegan who wasn't feeling well and decided to move away from veganism by adding just a bit of eggs and cheese to their diet. They stick to free-range eggs and certified-humane milk:

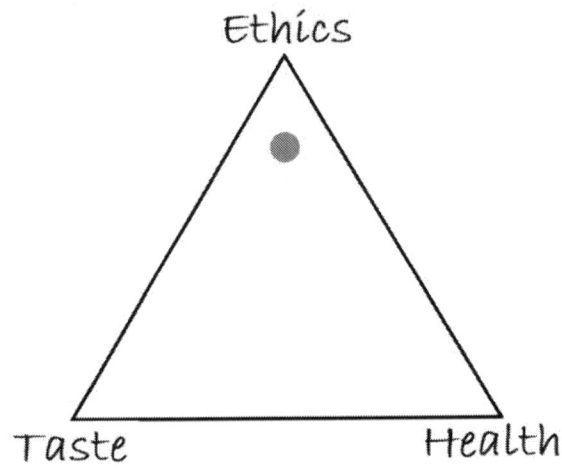

Here's the omnivore who has reduced his consumption of beef, chicken and fish, and insists on dolphin-safe tuna, free-range eggs, and locally-sourced organic produce.

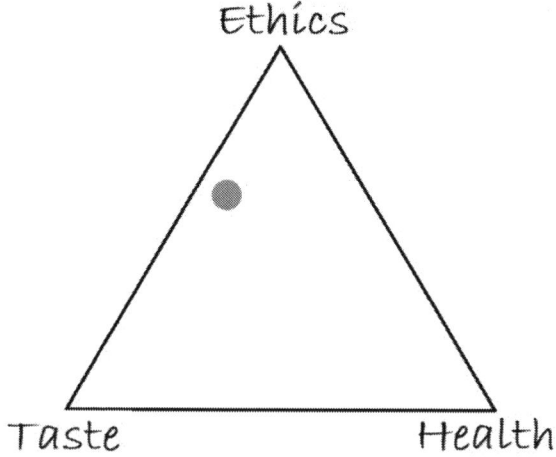

Here's a health nut who really tries to balance nuts, whole grains, rich flavors, moderate flesh consumption, and delicious French butter:

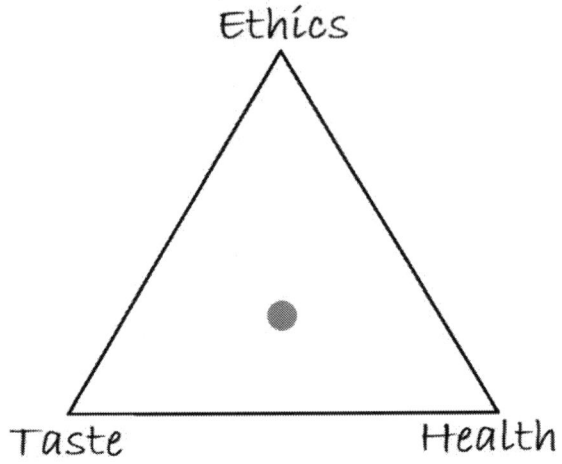

And here's the vegan who spends half of her life making amazing things out of beans, nuts, and whole grains.

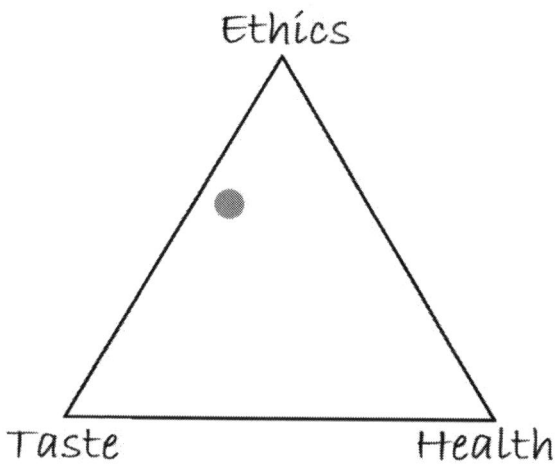

Actually, that dot can slide around quite a bit – there's a lot of subjectivity in plotting oneself on the triangle. Remember, it's personal and subjective, not mathematical and objective. Since this is more art than science, and how you eat is a personal choice, all you need is to have an approximate idea of where you are on this diagram, or where you'd like to be, and then be comfortable with your own balance between ethics, taste, and health.

Here's one that might surprise you: an omnivore who thinks it's perfectly ethical to eat animal flesh, and is careful about balanced diet, fat consumption, and sodium intake.

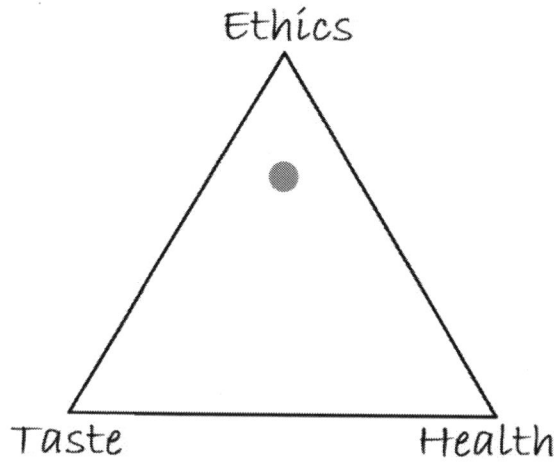

The double triplitarian triangle

A problem many of us face is the dichotomy between what we believe and what we practice. Call it weakness, call it honest acceptance of who we are, call it hypocrisy, it's part of human nature to…fail.

I believe that, with the possible exception of the Carnivore's Club, many of us find ourselves in the same boat as the guy who's not sure if he's a vegetarian in practice, though he might be one ethically. We think that there are ethical problems with some forms of consumption, but for reasons of weakness, health, laziness, desire, or economics, we are unable to achieve the diet that fits our ethical ideals.

For those people, which, based on a scientifically-determined wild-ass guess, is nearly everyone who is reading this, I provide the double triplitarian triangle. Not to be confused with the double helix, which is almost as interesting, the double triangle enables you to, through complex graphic manipulation, create a representation of how you'd like to consume, and what you actually consume.

To create this graphic for yourself, follow this complex procedure:

1. Make two copies of the triplitarian triangle, one to represent how you believe you should eat, and the other to represent how you actually eat.
2. Using a writing implement of your choice, plot a dot on each triangle.

Here's an example, based on my own attitudes:

Where I am, more or less:

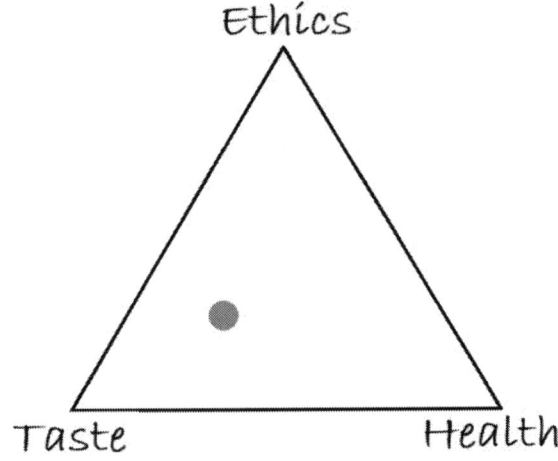

Where I'd like to be:

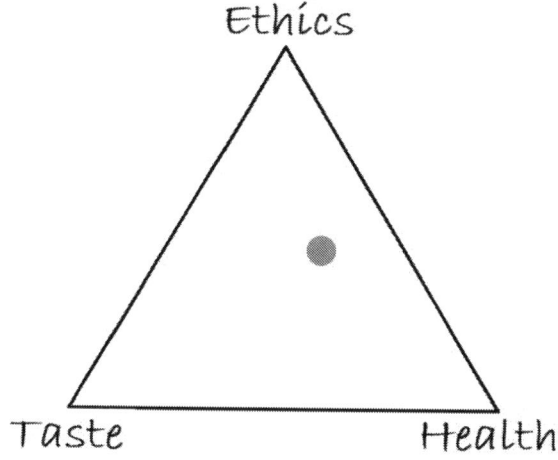

On observation, one could conclude that I kinda suck. Or maybe not. I have an internal conflict about eating flesh. I believe that nature meant for us to be omnivores. Nature abhors a vacuum, and a vegetarian. On the other hand, I feel for the animals. So, I do eat meat, chicken, and fish, but I also think about it, and frequently, feel bad about it. I consider whether eating a farm-raised chicken might be better than eating wild tuna. On the other hand, when I see a truck carrying a few hundred chickens to the slaughterhouse, I'm tempted to swear off meat, chicken, and fish.

Sometimes, I tilt more toward where my heart wants me to be and I order a lunch that's right over here:

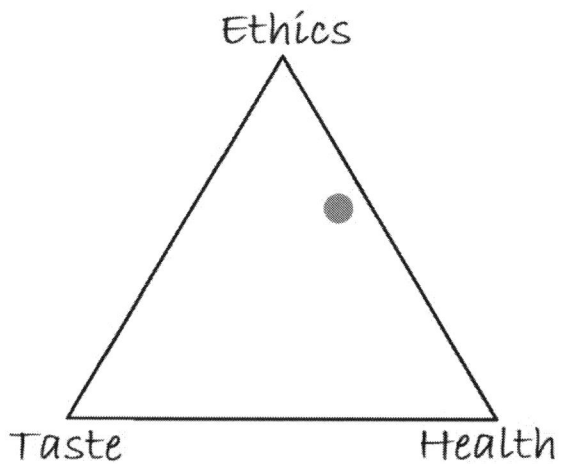

That's a salad of cucumbers, tomatoes, chick peas, croutons, and a hard-boiled egg, smothered in tahini. Delicious, by the way. A couple of slices of whole-grain bread slathered in butter and you're all set. Now that I think about it, I enjoy it more than the diagram indicates.

You can plot yourself on one triangle, plot your better self on a second triangle, and plot a meal or specific food items on yet a third triangle. Let's try it out on other foods.

Fois gras and veal:

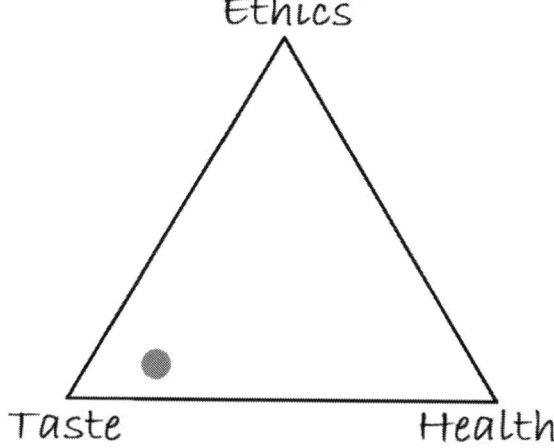

Eggs:

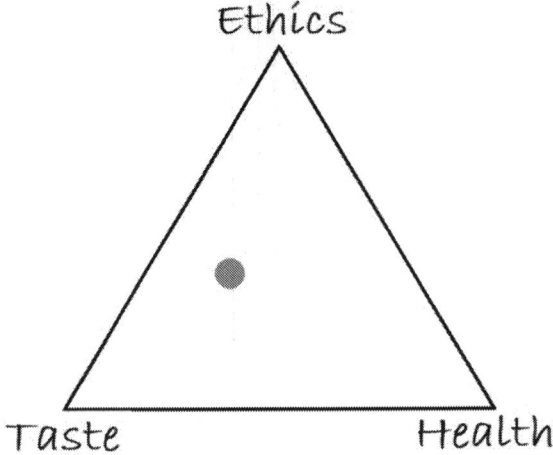

The implication that eggs are not so healthy may be wrong. Ask your doctor.

Free-range eggs:

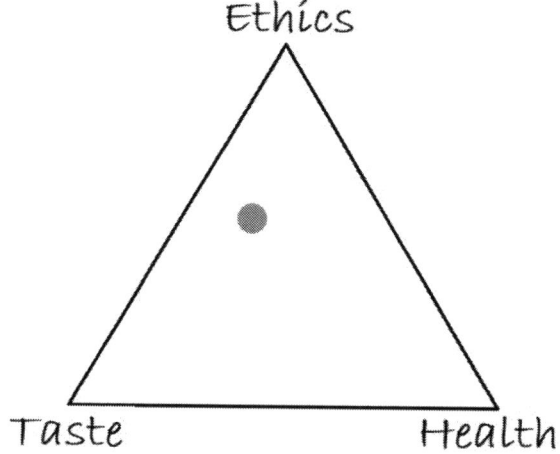

Here's a single triangle for wild-caught tuna and farm raised, free-range chicken:

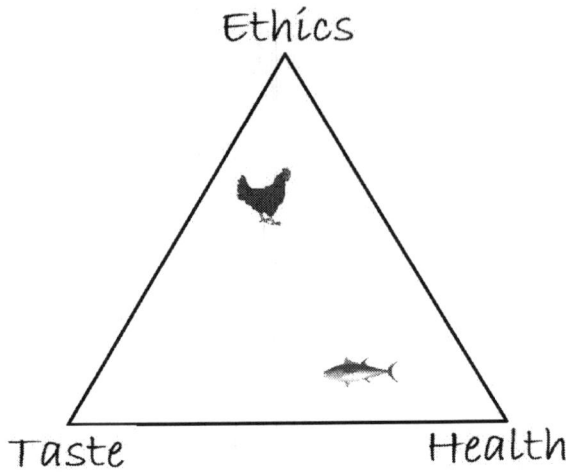

This triangle provides an easy-to-read graphic representation of how health, taste and ethics balance out for these two foods. The taste aspect is subjective, of course, but it seems that the destruction of whole populations of wild fish puts farm-raised chicken in a higher position on the ethical scale.

I try to pretend here that the chicken is a little less healthy than the tuna, but who knows, what with mercury contamination of the seas, and its presence in the sea food chain. "Ah ha," you say, "But what about all of the hormones and antibiotics that poultry producers feed their chickens?" To which I say, do a little research and make a decision. At some point, you might need to have some trust in your government (yes, government) to regulate the commercial food supply. See [this article](https://www.bestfoodfacts.org/farm-raised-chickens-hormones-antibiotics/) about chicken health and human health as a starting point.

So, use the triangle to define who you are, who you want to be, and what you're going to have for lunch. But for God's sake, don't talk about it – just tell everyone that you're a triplitarian.

Practical implications of being a triplitarian

Far be it from me to tell anyone how to eat. I don't know more than you do. But that's never stopped me before, so here are some suggestions that will change your life. Maybe.

Start by making a triplitarian triangle for a food item or for your own attitudes and practices. You're likely to be doing this in your head already, but having a formulation for understanding your attitudes and why you're eating the way you are may help you comprehend your choices, and then, relax.

Once you've clarified your position, you can stop talking about food choices all of the time. The triangle also provides a neat shortcut for summarizing your attitudes and practices, so that you can shut the Hell up about those food choices, and neatly brush off the annoying questions of your so-called friends. You can carry a mini-triangle in your pocket, and if the subject of food habits comes up, just flash it – though that's a little nerdy, I admit. And if someone mentions gluten, quickly change the subject.

At worst, you can use Ethics, Taste, and Health as a convenient shorthand. Here are some examples:

"I've been eating a lot of beef lately and it's making me feel a little sick and a little sad. I think I'll have the stir fry with tofu."

"I'm leaning away from ethics and toward taste tonight – bring on the steak."

Triangulating your way to moderation

Extreme opinions and recommendations about food, amplified by the media and social networks, pull us in opposing directions. My experience is that, with time, the pull in opposing directions puts me right in the middle, which makes some sense.

However, I recognize that not every person is as strong, or maybe, as apathetic, as I am.

In matters of food, moderation can work for many of us. Furthermore, *your* moderation should be guided by your own beliefs, attitudes, health needs, food preferences, and budget. Your choices should not be guided by magazine articles or books – not even this one.

For example, you may be wealthy enough to allow yourself to eat beef three or four times a day. But it might not be that healthy, and after a while it wouldn't even be enjoyable, so you may decide to have beef once a day, or four times a week. If you happen to have some ethical leanings toward vegetarianism, you might move to having beef one time a week.

Respect to those who try, but some of you are not doing well on a vegan diet. If you're a vegan, and your health starts to slide, consider eating a free-range egg every now and then, and a glass of milk might not be a bad idea - unless you're lactose-intolerant. If an egg is an ethical anathema to you, you can assuage your conscience by careful choice of your dairy and egg sources, making sure that they are sourced from animals that are well-treated. From a health perspective, it really, truly, takes a serious effort to live healthfully on a diet completely free of meat, dairy, and egg. Here's another great idea – see a dietician or a doctor.

And watch out for some of those meat-substitute soy and gluten products. Read the ingredients, and keep a chemistry reference nearby.

> *Ethical Anathema would be a good name for a band.*

An average omnivore could decide to move to free-range eggs to push the egg industry toward more ethical treatment of chickens, or to farm-raised fish to protect wild fish populations. Another omnivore might decide to buy the cheapest eggs and send the price difference to an organization that feeds the truly poor of other countries.

Those varied approaches have one thing in common — conscious consideration of important factors to arrive at a reasonable, non-fanatical decision.

Here's a few more ways to moderate, if you've been sucked in to a fanatical food fad.

Carbophobes should just chill. Eat some carbs. If you must, try to eat whole-grain carbs rather than bleached, white-flour carbs. But don't be a jerk about it. And enjoy sugar in moderation, unless your doctor tells you to lay off.

Carnivores and omnivores should at least be aware that meat, pork, chicken, fish, and shellfish come from living creatures. You're aware but have decided that it doesn't matter? Bon appétit!

Attention Glutenophobes! Most of us can eat gluten, and should at every opportunity. Gluten is the glue that sticks the wheat-eating world together. More plainly, it makes bread, bagels, and pizza chewy and delicious. If you're not really sensitive to gluten, eat some. If you think you are, see a doctor. Not just any doctor – a good one.

Same for MSGphobes. I'm personally not a fan of chemical additives, but a little bit here and there for those of us who are unaffected by MSG shouldn't be that big a deal.

Margarinophobes have it pretty easy. There are reasonable substitutes for margarine. Butter comes to mind. And for vegans, there's coconut oil. But there's no need to run screaming from a cookie that contains margarine. Run screaming because it contains sugar.

Acceptable and unacceptable food conversations

You don't have to be completely silent about food. On the other hand, you may not be able to tell which food conversations are verboten. Therefore, as a public service, I'm proud to present to you these examples of acceptable and unacceptable food conversations.

Scene 1: "Crème brûlée"
Location: A café in Paris
Henri: I really like the crème brûlée here.
Antoinette: Me too. It has a strong vanilla flavor.
Jean-Robert: Oh-la-la.
Ruling: Acceptable

Scene 2: Service fail
Location: A pancake house in Middle America

Bob: What happened to our waiter? I want to get the check and leave for work.

Bill: I don't know. The service has been slow here all day. And he didn't refill our water or our coffee.

Bob: I probably shouldn't leave a tip.

Bill: Leave something, it's a shit job.

Ruling: Acceptable

Scene 3: Tub of white meat chicken

Location: The office

Charlene: What have you got in that container?

Mike: That's boiled, boneless chicken breast. Because of my body-building, weight-training regimen, I need to consume 40 grams of lean protein every 3 hours. I also drink a whey-based protein drink, and eat protein bars with a low glycemic index. I wake up at 5 AM every morning to do two hours of weight training. That means I go to sleep at 9 every night, but it's worth it, because I...

Charlene: zzzzzzzzzzzzzzzzzzzzzzzzzzzzzzzzzz

Ruling: Unacceptable

Scene 4: Free-range, steak-fried chicken
Location: Denny's
Waitress: Today's special is free-range, steak-fried chicken, served with a side of free-range, chicken-fried steak.
Customer: Yum
Ruling: Acceptable

Scene 5: Gluten
Betsy: I don't eat gluten, I find that I feel much better without it, and when I discovered that I could buy gluten-free kielbasa…
Rachel: How 'bout this weather, bitch?
Ruling: Nice one, Rachel!

Scene 6: Tuna comes from tunas
Location: Picnic
Ben (mouth full of tuna salad sandwich): I'm a vegetarian.
Sally: You know that tuna comes from tunas, right?
Ben: Oops
Ruling: What an idiot

Scene 7: Herbs are murder
Location: Psychiatrist's office

Brendon: Herbs killed my mother
Psychiatrist: How does that make you feel?
Ruling: Get serious

My plan

My personal triplitarian plan is to reduce my meat consumption, because I feel sympathy, or perhaps, empathy, for the creatures I've been using as a food source. Put more simply, I feel bad about the animals that have to die so that I can eat.

Perhaps I'll become a finsemanaomnivore (FSO), a soon-to-be-household word I just made up that means *omnivore on the weekend*, and implies vegetarianism during the week, as well as a lousy ability to invent words. I'll make a bigger effort to buy free-range everything. And now that I'm done writing this book, I'll shut up about it. Unless I come up with a better word, such as…WochenendeAllesfresser?

Last words

Enjoy your food.
Stay well.
Be good.

Shut up and eat.

Acknowledgement

Thank you Rachel for your love and support, and for reviewing this work. All that is good here is material I adjusted or created anew because of your comments. Where it sucks, it's my own damn fault.

Made in the USA
Lexington, KY
30 November 2019